Censorship:
A Guide for Successful Workshop Planning

by Linda Schexnaydre, Nancy Burns,
and Emporia State University School of Library and
Information Management

ORYX PRESS
1984

The rare Arabian Oryx is believed to have inspired the myth of the unicorn. This desert antelope became virtually extinct in the early 1960s. At that time several groups of international conservationists arranged to have 9 animals sent to the Phoenix Zoo to be the nucleus of a captive breeding herd. Today the Oryx population is over 400 and herds have been returned to reserves in Israel, Jordan, and Oman.

Copyright © 1984 by The Oryx Press
2214 North Central at Encanto
Phoenix, Arizona 85004

Published simultaneously in Canada

Printed and Bound in the United States of America

Library of Congress Cataloging in Publication Data

Schexnaydre, Linda.
   Censorship, a guide for successful workshop planning.

   Bibliography: p.
   Includes index.
   1. Libraries—Censorship—Handbooks, manuals, etc.
2. Censorship—Handbooks, manuals, etc.   3. Freedom of information—Handbooks, manuals, etc.   4. Library institutes and workshops—Handbooks, manuals, etc.
I. Burns, Nancy, 1944–   .   II. Emporia State University. School of Library and Information Management.
III. Title.
Z711.4.S34   1984   025.2′13   83-43209
ISBN 0-89774-093-9

To Mildred Boyersmith, for her
enthusiastic support during the Censorship Workshops.

Contents

■ How to Use This Guide ■

Censorship: A Guide for Successful Workshop Planning provides complete directions for conducting a one-day workshop on censorship in libraries, including procedures for handling complaints about library materials. It is for public and school library media specialists, library and school board members, teachers, and administrators. The guide includes the necessary handouts, publicity materials, and training techniques. Also provided are ideas on how to organize the planning details—setting time and date, finding a location, identifying speakers, and making local arrangements. This workshop can be conducted for public library staff members, school personnel, or groups that include staff from all types of libraries. In a public library setting, it is important to include library board members, any Friends of the Library groups, and interested citizens, as well as public library staff. In a school setting, school library media specialists, teachers, building-level administrators, and district-level staff, as well as school board members, volunteers, and other interested persons, should be invited.

Part I gives you all the information you need for planning the workshop, including setting up a planning committee; deciding on workshop content; and preparing a budget, timeline for getting things done, and publicity materials.

Conducting the workshop is presented in Part II. This includes the purpose and objectives of the workshop, as well as instructions for the workshop staff; techniques to be used; and tips on room set-up, using handouts, and displays. A detailed, step-by-step outline of the actual workshop completes this section.

This basic workshop can also be modified to fit your training needs. You can use some of the ideas to produce a conference program at a local or state association conference. You can expand the workshop to become a one- or two-day statewide conference on censorship. You can conduct a staff development session for the staff of one library, media center, or library system. You can design an in-service training session for a school district. Part III gives specific suggestions for modifying or expanding the workshop design, including activities that may be substituted for, or added to, those described in the basic workshop in Part II. Parts IV and V include resources and transparencies which are ready to be duplicated for use at the workshop.

This guide assumes that the speakers will know about intellectual freedom issues pertinent to libraries and that the workshop coordinator will have some experience in planning and conducting workshops. If you need more information about intellectual freedom, consult the bibliographies found throughout Part III. One excellent source is *Defusing Censorship: The Librarian's Guide to Handling Censorship Conflicts* by Frances M. Jones (Phoenix, AZ: Oryx Press, 1983).

For those who want more information about organizing the details of a workshop, consult: "Can You Hear Me at the Back of the Room?" by A. James Challis and Brian Alley, *Technicalities*, vol. 2 (July 1982), pp. 12–15; *Cheap CE: Providing Continuing Education with Limited Resources: A Practical Guide* by Linda Waddle (Chicago: American Library Association, Young Adult Services Division, 1981); and *Planning Library Workshops and Institutes* by Ruth Warncke (Chicago: American Library Association, 1976).

For those who want more information about how to organize effective learning for adults and how to use different training techniques, see: *Planning, Conducting, Evaluating Workshops* by Larry Davis (Austin, TX: Learning Concepts, 1974).

The basic intellectual freedom workshop in this guide was originated in 1982 while the authors were on the faculty of the Emporia State University School of Library Science. It was produced under contract with the South Central Kansas Library System headquartered in Hutchinson, Kansas. The workshop was field tested with public library staff members, library board members, school library media specialists, Friends of the Library groups, and teachers. Suggestions from these participants and information from the workshop evaluation forms have been used to improve the workshop design.

Part I
Planning the Workshop

Planning Committee and Workshop Coordinator

In planning an intellectual freedom workshop, you should have a planning committee of from three to five people to help you make decisions about workshop content and planning details. Members of the planning committee should represent the sponsor(s) and also the audience for the workshop. You will want someone on the planning committee with some experience in coordinating workshops and someone who is knowledgeable about intellectual freedom issues as these relate to your particular workshop audience. These people could be from within the group, or you can contact:

> Intellectual freedom committee member from the state library association
> State library consultant
> State education agency consultant
> Library system consultant
> School district media supervisor
> Library school faculty member

For example, if the school district wants to sponsor a district-wide workshop for school library media specialists, teachers, and administrators, be sure that all of these groups are represented on the planning committee. Also include someone from the school district, possibly the district-level media supervisor.

One person should be designated as the workshop coordinator. The workshop coordinator will guide the work of the planning committee, will delegate tasks before and during the workshop, and will be responsible for coordinating the workshop itself.

QUESTIONS TO ANSWER

Here are some of the questions the planning committee needs to discuss during its first few meetings:

1. Will the workshop focus on public library issues or school issues or both?
2. What groups will be included as participants?
   - Public library staff
   - School library media specialists
   - Teachers
   - Public library board members
   - School administrators—building level and district level
   - Volunteers
   - Parents/PTA members

3. What are the major issues that need to be covered? What changes do you want to see following the workshop? Do participants need practice handling censorship complaints? Do they need to be briefed on the revised intellectual freedom statements from ALA? Or do they want to discuss their own concerns about the differences between selection guidelines and censorship?

4. Who will sponsor the workshop and what is the intended length of the training session?
   - One- or two-day statewide conference
   - One-day workshop for a school district or public library system
   - Two- to four-hour, or one-day staff development session or in-service training session for a local public library or a local school
   - Two-hour conference program at a state association meeting
   - Workshop sponsored by a library school, state library, or state education agency

5. Where will the workshop be held?
   - Individual library or school
   - State association conference site
   - Location that is centrally located and easily accessible within the school district or public library system
   - University with conference facilities that are centrally located

6. What is the most convenient time of the day and day of the week for the workshop?

▬ Workshop Content and Speakers ▬

Discuss the interests and training needs of your particular group to determine the content of the workshop. Carefully review the workshop design in Part II, as well as the ideas for modifications in Part III, and the handouts in Part IV. Make changes in the workshop design and workshop materials based on your local situation and the needs of the audience.

The planning committee will need to select a workshop leader to coordinate the entire workshop. The workshop leader should have experience working with groups and making presentations and should have some knowledge of the intellectual freedom issues that relate to your group. If you decide to use the workshop design as described in Part II of this manual, the workshop leader will lead role plays and group discussion. A workshop assistant should also be chosen to participate in role plays, to encourage group discussion, and to compile the results of the "Censorship Quiz." If role plays, as well as case studies and some of the other activities described in the basic workshop are not wanted, it is possible to substitute other activities. See Part III, "Alternate Workshop Ideas," for ideas.

The workshop, as described in Part II, features a speaker to give a keynote address on intellectual freedom (although the workshop can be modified so that no speaker is used). Be sure that this speaker understands and can speak on those aspects of intellectual freedom pertinent to your group. Here are some contacts for locating a speaker.

For public libraries:
Regional library system headquarters
State library
Intellectual freedom committee of the state
    library association
For school settings:
State department of education
State education association
State library association or state school library
    association
Regional educational service center
From your local area:
Lawyer
School board member or public library trustee
Director from a nearby school, media center,
    or public library
Faculty member from a nearby college or university
Library school faculty member

▬ Budget ▬

Consider the items on the budget worksheet that are applicable to your workshop. What will the costs be? To cut expenses, you may be able to get donations of supplies, food, and services from any sponsors, Friends of the Library, the PTA, or local businesses. The workshop staff may be willing to speak for reimbursement of their expenses and no honorarium. If you are going to charge a registration fee, total the expenses that need to be recovered, divide the cost by the anticipated number attending the workshop, and increase the fee by 20 percent to determine the total registration fee.

BUDGET WORKSHEET

Directions: List all expenses. Indicate what, if any, expenses are being paid for by specific groups. Check those expenses that need to be recovered (through registration fees).

	Expenses	Subtotals
1. Speakers		
Honoraria	_____	
Travel and lodging	_____	
Meals	_____	_____
2. Publicity		
Printing	_____	
Postage	_____	_____
3. Supplies		
Duplication of handouts	_____	
10 blank transparencies	_____	
Name tags	_____	
Folders for handouts	_____	
Newsprint and markers (optional)	_____	
Blank audiotape or videotape (to record the workshop)	_____	_____
4. Facility charges	_____	_____
5. Telephone expenses	_____	_____
6. Food		
Coffee/tea/juice	_____	
Refreshments	_____	
Lunch	_____	_____
7. Equipment rental		
Overhead projector	_____	
Screen	_____	
Other _____	_____	
_____	_____	_____
	Total:	_____

To determine the registration fee:

1. Total the expenses that need to be recovered from the registration fee. _____

2. Estimate the number of participants. _____

3. Divide the expenses (Line 1) by the number of participants (Line 2). _____

4. Multiply the number on Line 3 by 20 percent _____

5. Add Line 3 to Line 4 for the registration fee. _____

▬ **Timeline** ▬

The workshop coordinator and the planning committee should list what needs to be done before the workshop, decide who is responsible for each activity, and schedule these activities. The workshop coordinator is responsible for guiding the activities of the planning committee, seeing that all activities are completed on schedule, and reporting back to the committee if any plans need to be revised. The planning committee should continue to meet regularly before the workshop.

The following timeline includes major tasks that should be accomplished before the workshop. Three or four months should be enough time to plan a local or multi-county workshop based on the design in this manual. A statewide workshop, or a workshop that is more complex than the one described in this manual, will require more planning time. A small in-house workshop will probably require less time.

During the week following the workshop, the planning committee should meet to evaluate the workshop and to discuss the participant evaluations. What were the strengths and weaknesses of the workshop? Were the training objectives met? What would you do differently next time?

3 Months Ahead	Who?	**Target Date to Complete Task**
_____ Form planning committee and hold first meeting.	_____	_____
_____ Determine who the participants will be and what they need to learn.	_____	_____
_____ Determine workshop content and modify workshop design as needed.	_____	_____
_____ Develop budget. Decide how workshop expenses will be covered. Will there be a registration fee?	_____	_____
_____ Set date of workshop, avoiding conflicts with other events of interest to participants.	_____	_____
_____ Select location. Site must be large enough to seat estimated number of participants and easily accessible.	_____	_____
_____ Select keynote speaker and workshop leader.	_____	_____
_____ Announce date, location, workshop title, and brief description in newsletters targeted to participants.	_____	_____
_____ Prepare publicity/registration flyer.	_____	_____
_____ Make arrangements for printing and mailing of publicity/registration flyer.	_____	_____
_____ Order handouts from ALA (see Part IV) and other needed materials, such as films, videotapes, books, journal articles, etc. See Part III.	_____	_____

2 Months Ahead	**Who?**	**Target Date to Complete Task**
_____ Mail or distribute publicity/registration flyers.	_____	_____
_____ Decide what handouts to use from this manual. (See Part IV.) Which need to be revised? Which need to be compiled using local information?	_____	_____
_____ Prepare transparencies from the manual (Part V).	_____	_____
_____ Arrange for equipment at workshop site.	_____	_____
_____ Plan ''Banned Books'' display or other types of displays.	_____	_____
_____ Arrange for refreshments and lunch.	_____	_____
_____ Prepare local information about restaurants if lunch is not to be served at workshop.	_____	_____
_____ Locate volunteers to assist on the day of the workshop with registration, refreshments, and setting up the facilities.	_____	_____

1 Month Ahead	**Who?**	**Target Date to Complete Task**
_____ Set preregistration deadline one week before the workshop and process the preregistration forms as they are received.	_____	_____
_____ Send registrants a memo to confirm their registration. Include a map to workshop site and parking information.	_____	_____
_____ Print handouts based on estimated number of participants.	_____	_____
_____ Compile handouts into packets.	_____	_____
_____ Gather materials for the displays.	_____	_____
_____ Confirm number of participants one week before workshop for food and seating arrangements.	_____	_____
_____ Double check all arrangements at workshop site—equipment, food, seating.	_____	_____
_____ Double check with keynote speaker and workshop leader.	_____	_____
_____ Check with the planning committee to make sure that all assignments have been completed and that there are no last-minute problems.	_____	_____
_____ Compile registration list and make name tags (or participants can make their own name tags during registration).	_____	_____
_____ Make directional signs for outside the workshop site, for inside the building, and for the registration area. Be sure to put a sign on the meeting room door and the coffee break area.	_____	_____

■ Publicity

The planning committee will decide how to publicize the workshop. The strategies you select will vary depending on your audience. Discuss how you can best publicize the workshop to those you want to participate. Here are some ideas.

For local workshops:
- Posters in libraries, schools, other sites.
- Memo or publicity flyer distributed to staff and board members.
- News items in staff newsletter.
- Article in local newspaper.

For library system or school district:
- Publicity flyer mailed or distributed to staff in libraries and schools in the area.
- News items in the school district or library system newsletter.
- Article in newspaper of city hosting workshop and other cities if appropriate.

For statewide workshop:
- Publicity flyer mailed to public libraries, school library media centers, and schools in the state.
- Publicity flyer mailed to members of the state library association, state school library association, and/or state education association.
- News items in state library or state education association newsletter.
- News item in regional library system newsletters.
- News item in school district newsletters.
- News item in state library association or state education association newsletter.
- Article in newspaper of city hosting workshop or in newspaper with statewide readership.

See the following pages for a sample press release, a sample publicity flyer with preregistration form, and a memo to workshop participants (to be mailed on receipt of the preregistration form).

SAMPLE PRESS RELEASE

Use this press release to send to city newspapers, school or library newsletters, school district or library system newsletters, state library or state education department newsletters, or state library association or state education association newsletters.

August 1, 1984

FOR IMMEDIATE RELEASE

For further information, contact:

Joan Hartman
South Central Library System
123 W. Main
Anytown, KS 67000
(999) 222-3344

WORKSHOP ON CENSORSHIP AND INTELLECTUAL FREEDOM

Public librarians, school library media specialists, and teachers are invited to attend a workshop on censorship and intellectual freedom Friday, October 5, 1984, from 8:30 a.m. to 3:30 p.m. at the Henry Branch Library, Anytown, Kansas. The $5 registration fee includes lunch. Sponsored by the South Central Library System and the Smithville School District, the one-day workshop will focus on practical techniques for dealing with censorship problems in schools and public libraries. Content includes: basic principles of intellectual freedom, building support in the community and with governing bodies, writing sample policies, developing procedures for handling complaints, and dealing with citizen complaints.

Public library staff members, library trustees, school library media specialists, teachers, and school administrators are encouraged to attend as teams so that they can work together on policies and procedures to improve their local situations.

Workshop leaders are Richard Wood, director of the Smithville Public Library, and Linda Webster, president of the Smithville Board of Education.

For more information and registration materials, contact Joan Hartman, South Central Library System, 123 W. Main, Anytown, KS 67000, (999) 222-3344. The deadline for preregistration is September 28, 1984.

SAMPLE PUBLICITY/REGISTRATION FLYER

CENSORSHIP AND INTELLECTUAL FREEDOM—A WORKSHOP FOR PUBLIC AND SCHOOL LIBRARIANS

Sponsored by the South Central Library System
and the Smithville School District

DATE: Friday, October 5, 1984

TIME: 9:00 a.m. to 3:30 p.m. (Registration 8:30 a.m.–9 a.m.)

PLACE: Henry Branch Library
1234 Central
Anytown, KS

COST: $5 includes handouts, refreshments, and lunch
(to be paid on the day of the workshop)

This workshop provides practical techniques for dealing with censorship problems, particularly in public and school libraries.

Come to learn about:
- Basic principles of intellectual freedom
- Building support in your community and with your governing body
- Writing policies and developing procedures for handling citizen complaints
- Dealing with citizen complaints

Workshop Leaders:
- Richard Wood, Director, Smithville Public Library
- Linda Webster, President, Smithville Board of Education

DETACH

Return to: Joan Hartman, South Central Library System, 123 W. Main, Anytown, KS 67000, (999) 222-3344. Deadline is September 28, 1984.

Yes, I plan to attend the **Intellectual Freedom Workshop.**

NAME:_____

ADDRESS:_____
_____

LIBRARY OR SCHOOL:_____

My major concerns in the area of intellectual freedom: _____
_____
_____

Briefly describe any experiences you've had in dealing with citizen complaints about library materials. (Continue on the back of this form if necessary.) _____
_____
_____

SAMPLE MEMO TO PARTICIPANTS

September 25, 1984

TO: Participants for the workshop on Censorship and Intellectual Freedom

FROM: Joan Hartman, South Central Library System

RE: Upcoming workshop

Welcome to the workshop on "Censorship and Intellectual Freedom." I'm pleased that you have chosen to attend, and I look forward to seeing you during the workshop.

The workshop will be held at the Henry Branch Library, 1234 Central, Anytown, Kansas. Registration is from 8:30–9:00 a.m. Coffee and doughnuts will be served. I've enclosed a map indicating the location of the library and parking across the street. There are several motels with restaurants within walking distance of the Henry Branch Library.

Ramada Inn, 1145 Central, Anytown, KS 67000 (999) 222-5498

Holiday Inn, 989 Main, Anytown, KS 67000 (999) 222-3879

Downtowner, 750 Main, Anytown, KS 67000 (999) 222-4567

All have agreed to give discount rates to workshop participants.

We hope that several people from your library or school will be able to attend. This would be a particularly good opportunity to involve members of your public library board or your local board of education.

If you have any questions, don't hesitate to contact me.

Joan Hartman
South Central Library System
123 W. Main
Anytown, KS 67000
(999) 222-3344

Part II
Conducting the Workshop

Purpose and Objectives

PURPOSE

This workshop provides basic intellectual freedom principles and practical techniques for dealing with censorship problems in schools and public libraries. It is designed for public library staff members, public library trustees, Friends of the Library groups, school library media specialists, teachers, school administrators, parents, and interested citizens.

OBJECTIVES

After the workshop, participants will:

1. Be able to discuss the basic principles of intellectual freedom as they relate to their specific situations.

2. Identify two new ideas to build support for intellectual freedom in their community and with their governing board.

3. Be able to draft or revise a written selection policy statement for their library and develop or revise written procedures for handling citizen complaints.

4. Be able to integrate revised ALA intellectual freedom statements into existing library policy.

5. Identify two sources for help when censorship problems occur.

6. Be able to handle citizen complaints about library materials more effectively.

■ Staff and Techniques Needed for Conducting the Workshop ■

WORKSHOP STAFF

You will need three workshop staff members:

1. The workshop leader is responsible for the content of the entire workshop. S/he should have experience in leading group discussion, be comfortable with doing role plays, and be able to briefly lecture about the importance of materials selection policies and procedures for handling citizen complaints. S/he will also need to be familiar with the ALA statements on intellectual freedom.

2. The keynote speaker should speak for 45 minutes on intellectual freedom principles pertinent to public libraries or the school system (or both), intellectual freedom statements prepared by national organizations such as the American Library Association and the National Council of Teachers of English, and building community support for intellectual freedom. S/he will answer questions following the speech.

3. The workshop assistant will role play with the workshop leader, help facilitate group discussion, assist groups in working on their case studies, and compile the results of the "Censorship Quiz."

WORKSHOP TECHNIQUES

This workshop uses a variety of techniques to encourage active participation and to increase interest in learning. The keynote speech and handouts provide basic information about intellectual freedom. Role plays, case studies, and group discussion encourage participation from the group. The workshop is scheduled tightly. If you have a large group of people or if you want to increase time for discussion, lengthen some of the activities or shorten the keynote address. You can also shorten the noon break if lunch is served at the workshop site. See Part III for ideas on activities that can be substituted for the keynote speaker, role plays, and/or case studies that are described in the basic workshop in Part II.

Role Plays

Role plays are used to demonstrate common difficulties in handling citizen complaints. Demonstration role plays are done by the workshop leader and the workshop assistant in front of the group. Participants are not asked to do role plays, since this is often an uncomfortable way for people to try out new behavior. Workshop staff should practice the role plays a few times before the workshop to get an idea of how each approaches the situation. But the strength of role plays is their unrehearsed quality—so don't try to memorize lines or expect that you'll do the role play exactly the same each time. Also don't worry that you may do something wrong. The benefit of a role play is that participants can point out what you do well and what you need to improve. Often mistakes or unexpected situations are very instructive to the group. If you get stuck in the middle of a role play, "cut" the action and ask the group what they suggest you do next. Don't get bogged down in the role play. Discuss what happened and what should have happened and move on to the next role play or the next part of the agenda.

Case Studies

Case studies are used with small groups so participants can practice their strategies for handling citizen complaints in a specific situation. You can ask participants to bring in actual censorship problems that concern them but have some case studies available for groups that do not have actual situations to work on. Be sure that you give clear directions to the groups and that you let them know how much time they have to work. (Directions for this activity are in instructions for conducting the workshop, pp. 30–31). Each group will select a reporter to note the group's responses to the questions included at the end of each case study. The reporter will also act as group leader and timekeeper to see that the group focuses its discussion and that it completes its task on time. Timing is very important. You need to give the groups enough time to complete the task but not so much time that they become bored with the experience.

Group Discussion

Group discussion is also an important part of this workshop. Intellectual freedom involves controversial and complex issues. Libraries may have somewhat different approaches, policies, and procedures. Participants may have different attitudes and interpretations. Talking about these issues can be very stressful. You will want to give participants a chance to air their feelings, their fears, their discouragements, and their difficulties, as well as their good ideas. However, you don't want the workshop to deteriorate into endless recountings of "what happened in my library" or into situations where participants criticize the procedures or decisions of other members of the group. Although some participants may choose to strengthen their stand on intellectual freedom as a result of the workshop, participants should not feel threatened or judged by other group members. It is difficult to learn and to risk change in an atmosphere where group members criticize each other or other libraries. The workshop leader should be particularly sensitive to this. Suggestions are acceptable; criticism is not.

You may also notice a tendency for the group to discount, ridicule, or criticize people in the community who do not share their values regarding intellectual freedom. "Censor" is a strong label that librarians can use to rally support. However, remind the group to respect the complainant's right to his/her own opinion and values and to respect his/her right as a citizen to lodge a complaint.

Here are some specific tips to improve group discussion:

1. Listen to what people are saying. Ask questions to clarify points not fully expressed.

2. Don't assume that you have to answer all questions from the group. Redirect them to the group itself and see what opinions and alternatives emerge.

3. Let members of the group respond to each other. Don't feel you must comment after every statement.

4. Remember what you want the discussion to accomplish. Continue encouraging discussion with questions until you feel that all essential points have been identified. Remind the group of its focus if discussion begins to wander.

5. Watch for signs of fatigue and loss of attention and interest. Quickly summarize the essential points and begin the next activity.

6. Tell the group how much time you've allotted for discussion. Call time and summarize once the time is up. The workshop assistant could be the time-keeper.

7. You may wish to write the major points on a blank overhead transparency, a chalkboard, or a flip chart during the discussion and refer to these points during your summary. The workshop assistant could do the writing to allow you to lead the discussion more easily.

Physical Arrangements

ROOM SET-UP

Arrange the room with rows of chairs facing the front, either in straight rows or in a semi-circle. A center aisle is useful. At the front of the room, put a table with a lectern (if desired) and two or three chairs for the workshop staff. The morning session can be held in an auditorium, but the afternoon session involves small group work which requires chairs that can be arranged in small circles.

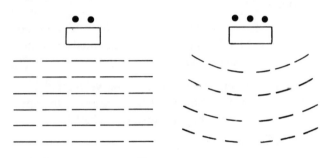

Additional Furniture

- One table for refreshments
- One table for registration and packets
- One or more tables for displays

Equipment and Supplies

- Overhead projector
- Screen
- Extension cord(s)
- Seven blank transparencies (unless flip chart or chalkboard is used)
- Marking pens for transparencies
- Transparency of the ''Intellectual Freedom Questionnaire'' (Part V)
- Transparency of the ''Censorship Quiz'' (Part V)

Optional Equipment and Supplies

- Other audiovisual equipment if films, slides, filmstrips, audiocassettes, or videocassettes are used
- Flip chart and easel with markers (rather than overhead transparencies—copy material from transparency masters in Part V onto flip charts before workshop starts)
- Chalkboard and chalk (rather than overhead transparencies—have material from Part V already written on board before workshop starts)
- Microphone and amplifier if room is large or if acoustics are poor

■ Workshop Materials ■

This manual includes all materials needed for the workshop (see Part IV), except for some of the intellectual freedom statements that can be ordered directly from the American Library Association. Note which materials need to be modified to fit your particular workshop, which need to be compiled using local information, and which need to be ordered. You may reproduce, for workshop participants, worksheets and handouts in this manual without further permission from the publisher, as long as such reproductions are used for nonprofit, educational purposes and not sold or used in other publications.

LIST OF RESOURCES

The following handouts should be available in packets for each participant:

Participant's Agenda (modify)
List of Local Restaurants (if necessary)
Intellectual Freedom Questionnaire
Censorship Quiz
ALA Statements*
 1. "Library Bill of Rights"—reprinted in this manual
 2. "The Freedom to Read"—reprinted in this manual
 3. "Intellectual Freedom Statement"
 4. "Evaluating Library Collections"
 5. "Free Access to Libraries for Minors"
 6. "Restricted Access to Library Materials"
 7. "Statement on Labeling"
 8. "Policy on Confidentiality of Library Records"
 9. "Exhibit Spaces and Meeting Rooms"
 10. "Diversity in Collection Development"
 11. "Dealing with Concerns about Library Resources"

 12. "Expurgation of Library Materials"
 13. "Library Initiated Programs as a Resource"
 14. "Administrative Policies and Procedures Affecting Access to Library Resources and Services"
"Freedom to View"
"The Students' Right to Read"**
Selection Policies (choose for school library media center or public library)
Request for Reconsideration of Library Materials
Procedures for Reconsideration of Library Materials
4 Case Studies (one per participant)
Case Study Summaries
What to Do in Your Community
Where to Get Help (compile)
For More Information
Especially for Public Libraries
Especially for Schools
Workshop Evaluation Form

ADDITIONAL RESOURCES

Buttons with the slogan "I Read Banned Books" are available from American Society of Journalists and Authors, 1501 Broadway, Suite 1907, New York, NY 10036. The cost is $1 each for orders of 1 to 100 buttons and $.50 each for orders of 101 to 1,000 buttons.

T-shirts listing frequently challenged books are available from the Washington Coalition Against Censorship. *Diary of a Young Girl,* by Anne Frank; *In the Night Kitchen,* by Maurice Sendak; and other titles are printed with a "censored" stamp across them diagonally. White on navy, royal blue, burgundy, or lavender, in small, medium, large, or extra large. Order for $8.00 plus $1.00 mailing from WCAC, 2101 Smith Tower, Seattle, WA 98104.

*Available for purchase from Office for Intellectual Freedom, American Library Association, 50 E. Huron St., Chicago, IL 60611, (312) 944-6780. Many ALA statements are also reprinted in *Defusing Censorship: The Librarian's Guide to Handling Censorship Conflicts* by Frances M. Jones (Phoenix, AZ: Oryx Press, 1983), pp. 157–91. In addition, state intellectual freedom handbooks contain the ALA intellectual freedom statements. Contact your state library association, state education association, state library, or state department of education to see if your state has such a handbook.

**The entire statement is available in booklet form for $.25 from National Council of Teachers of English, 1111 Kenyon Road, Urbana, IL 61801, (217) 328-3870.

■ **Displays** ■

You may want to display books that have been banned throughout the years and books that are currently controversial in schools and public libraries. There are a number of resources for developing a banned books display.

"Banned Book Exhibit." Available from Office for Intellectual Freedom, American Library Association, 50 E. Huron St., Chicago, IL 60611. (312) 944-6780.

A collection of 60 books banned in United States libraries from 1976 to 1981, which includes books, laminated 3″ × 5″ cards describing the censorship incident, and a notebook containing more detailed information. This is free except for shipping charges; however, it could take up to one year to schedule it in your area. The Office for Intellectual Freedom has additional copies of all the above materials excluding the books which can be loaned with a shorter waiting period.

"*Banned Books Week*" *Materials*. Available from Office for Intellectual Freedom, American Library Association, 50 E. Huron St., Chicago, IL 60611. (312) 944-6780.

The Banned Books Week kit for 1983 includes a poster, a list of books that have been challenged or banned during 1982–83, camera-ready art for ads and bookmarks, display ideas, and a sample news release. Inquire about availability and cost.

De Grazia, Edward, and Newman, Roger K. *Banned Films: Movie Censorship in the United States*. New York: Bowker, 1982.

History of film censorship in the United States from 1908 to 1981, with detailed information about the 122 films that were banned.

Haight, Anne Lyon. *Banned Books: 387 B.C. to 1978 A.D.*, 4th ed. New York: Bowker, 1978.

A chronological list of banned books with information on the controversy surrounding them, as well as excerpts from important court cases and selected U.S. laws and regulations.

Jones, Frances M. *Defusing Censorship: The Librarian's Guide to Handling Censorship Conflicts*. Phoenix, AZ: Oryx Press, 1983. Appendix 3 (pp. 193–209).

"Banned Books," is a list of censored books compiled by the American Booksellers Association.

"List of Books Some People Consider Dangerous." Chicago: American Library Association, Office for Intellectual Freedom, 1983.

A 37-page annotated list of controversial books.

Newsletter on Intellectual Freedom. Bimonthly. Chicago: American Library Association.

Useful for information about materials currently causing complaints in schools and public libraries.

You may also want to display materials from your state intellectual freedom groups. You will have identified these sources on the handout "Where to Get Help" (Part IV).

RULES

1. The chairperson of the Review Committee is officially in charge. Observers may speak by first standing to be recognized by the chairperson.

2. Either the Committee on Decency or the Review Committee may call for a caucus to realign its strategies at any time.

3. The game leaders may direct either committee to draw chance cards at any time.

10 min. Simulation begins. Mrs. Hilmer, with the assistance of the game leader, will present the objectionable material. The example *Blackboard, Blackboard on the Wall, Who Is the Fairest One of All?* is presented in a slide/tape of the illustrations and narration; however, game leaders may wish to use other methods of presentation.

10 min. Participants move into physical arrangement most conducive for simulation. The arrangement might be as follows with the Review Committee at the front of the room:

Review Committee

Observers—
Committee on
Decency

Observers—
Supporters of
Intellectual
Freedom

The Review Committee and the Committee on Decency meet separately. Observers may join the committee they support. Members become acquainted with each other's roles, the selection policy, and the complaint form Mrs. Hilmer has submitted. Each group needs to plan its strategy; however, chance cards will be pulled periodically. These cards may significantly alter the situation.

15 min. Chairperson of the Review Committee calls the meeting to order and then calls upon Mrs. Hilmer. She may comment on the the objectionable material and then turn the meeting over to the chairperson of the Committee on Decency for further comments. This meeting is called primarily to hear the issues presented by Mrs. Hilmer and the committee on Decency.

Meeting adjourned.

15 min. Chairperson of the Review Committee calls the second meeting to order. Committee on Decency is again in attendance, but the primary focus of this meeting is on the Review Committee. They review the information, discuss and make a recommendation concerning the future use of the book. Final judgment is not mandatory.

Meeting is adjourned.

10 min. Debriefing and discussion.

ROLES

Complainant: Mrs. Henry (Helen) Hilmer, elementary teacher.

Committee on Decency: a group of concerned citizens from Town A.

Chairman: Mr. Henry Hilmer, real estate agent.

Vice President: Mr. Bryce Nelson, farmer.

Secretary: Mrs. Wilma Simms, homemaker and mother.

Treasurer: Mr. Claus Jacobs, banker.

Members at large: Mrs. Virgil Black, senior citizen.
Mr. Daniel Drake, owner of auto repair business.

Other committee members may be present as indicated by their name tags. Supporting witnesses may be created from this group, e.g., Rev. David Beck, minister of the Southern Witness for the Free Evangelical Church.

Review Committee, selected on the basis of the Northeast-Southwest Community School District's Instructional Materials Selection Policy, is comprised of 3 students, 3 faculty members, and 5 community persons. Roles indicated (*) may be eliminated if there are fewer than 21 participants.

Chairperson: Mrs. Ann Buckley, homemaker and civic volunteer.

Secretary: Mr. James Henry, elementary principal at Town C.

Sally Mason, 9th grader.

*Dawn Kelly, a junior

Nathan Sauers, a senior.

Mrs. Yavonne Zimmer, homemaker and mother.

*Mrs. Becky Staley, junior high media specialist.

Mr. Dale McCormack, high school social studies teacher.

Rev. Ray Appleby, United Methodist minister.

Mr. Hank Lang, farmer.

*Mr. Eric Bussey, professional photographer.

Supporters of intellectual freedom are among the observers. Supporting witnesses may be created from this group, e.g., Mr. Tom Marshall, reporter for the *Des Moines Herald*.

Workshops for Public Libraries Only

For workshops geared to public library staff members, include public library trustees, Friends of the Library, volunteers, interested citizens, staff from the regional library system, and consultants from the state library. Discuss the following content areas:

1. Use of public meeting rooms.

2. Policy on displays.

3. Policy on library-sponsored speakers and programs.

4. Children's materials and children's access to library services.

5. Community education and public relations concerning intellectual freedom.

RESOURCES

The following resource materials will be particularly useful:

Broderick, Dorothy M. "Censorship: A Family Affair?" *Top of the News* 35 (Spring 1979): 223–32.

A discussion of societal values as these affect children's right to read.

————. *Library Work with Children*. New York: H. W. Wilson, 1977.

A resource that covers controversial issues in collection development for children's materials.

Bundy, Mary Lee, and Stakem, Teresa. "Librarians and Intellectual Freedom: Are Opinions Changing?" *Wilson Library Bulletin* 56 (Spring 1982): 584–89.

Results of a survey sent to public librarians about their attitudes toward intellectual freedom.

Jones, Frances M. *Defusing Censorship: The Librarian's Guide to Handling Censorship Conflicts*. Phoenix, AZ: Oryx Press, 1983.

Note especially Chapters 6—"Intellectual Freedom and Censorship in Public Libraries: The Rights of Library Users and Library Employees"; 7—"Public Library Censorship: Legal Issues"; 8—"Children's Access, 'Dangerous' Materials, and Other Concerns in Public Libraries"; 9—"Meeting Rooms, Exhibits, and Programs in the Library"; and Appendix 1—"Policies and Guidelines for Public Libraries."

■ Workshops on Children's Materials and Services ▬▬▬

If your group of school and/or public librarians is most interested in discussing children's access to information, materials, and services, the following resource materials will be useful:

RESOURCES

Broderick, Dorothy M. "Censorship: A Family Affair?" *Top of the News* 35 (Spring 1979): 223–32.

A discussion of family values and lifestyles as these affect children's right to read.

———. *Library Work with Children*. New York: H. W. Wilson, 1977.

Collection development for children's materials, including the controversy surrounding sexism and racism in children's books, sex and sexuality, and selection standards.

Coughlan, Margaret N. "Guardians of the Young: Why There Has Never Been—and Probably Never Will Be—Intellectual Freedom for Children." *Top of the News* 33 (Winter 1977): 137–48.

Historical survey of differing views of children's reading and children's right to information.

Jones, Frances M. *Defusing Censorship: The Librarian's Guide to Handling Censorship Conflicts*. Phoenix, AZ: Oryx Press, 1983.

Information about court cases on students' rights and public library policies on children's access.

MacLeod, Anne Scott. "Censorship and Children's Literature." *Library Quarterly* 53 (January 1983): 26–38.

A discussion of conflicts in current social attitudes toward childhood and children as these relate to censorship of books for the young.

Nelson, Eva. "Why We Hardly Have Any Picture Books in the Children's Department Anymore: A Brief Fantasy." *Top of the News* 28 (November 1972): 54–56.

A satire on an imaginary library which removes books automatically once a complaint is lodged.

Robotham, John, and Shields, Gerald. *Freedom of Access to Library Materials*. New York: Neal-Schuman, 1982.

A book that contains sections on the age at which children should have access to all materials and the special problems posed by materials deemed racist, sexist, ageist.

VOYA (Voice of Youth Advocates). Bimonthly, April through February. $15/year. Voice of Youth Advocates, P.O. Box 6569, University, AL 35486.

A periodical that includes articles on intellectual freedom for children and young adults and book reviews of materials in the areas of sexuality, realistic fiction, and nonfiction dealing with the day-to-day concerns of children and youth.

■■■ Workshops for Staff Development/ In-Service Training ■■■

An outline for a three-hour staff development session for public or school library staff can be found in *Defusing Censorship: The Librarian's Guide to Handling Censorship Conflicts* by Frances M. Jones (Phoenix, AZ: Oryx Press, 1983). See Appendix 5, "Inservice Training in Intellectual Freedom."

The chief strengths of this workshop are:

1. Discussion of the "Library Bill of Rights" and its "Interpretations."

2. Discussion of citizen questions, complaints, or objections to library materials.

3. Opportunity for participants to raise issues relating to their libraries.

■■■ Workshop on the Legal Interpretations of Obscenity ■■■

Your group may have a particular interest in the legal interpretations of obscenity. In this case, you can focus the morning session on recent court cases and the different Supreme Court definitions of obscenity. Lawyers and members of the local and state chapters of the American Civil Liberties Union are excellent resource people. Be sure to include speakers who are knowledgeable about your state's obscenity laws.

The questionnaire "Censorship: The Search for the Obscene" (see next page) can be substituted for either the "Censorship Quiz" or the "Intellectual Freedom Questionnaire." This will provide an opportunity to explore information and attitudes about what is defined as obscene.

RESOURCES

Following are resources that will help.

Bosmajian, Haig A. *Censorship, Libraries, and the Law*. New York: Neal-Schuman, 1983.

Lower court decisions about censorship in libraries as well as pertinent Supreme Court rulings.

Censorship Litigation and the Schools. Chicago: American Library Association, 1983.

Proceedings of a colloquium for lawyers, librarians, and publishers to analyze the opposition to First Amendment Rights, the proper duty of the state in shaping school curricula, and strategies for selecting and winning cases in the courts.

Jones, Frances M. *Defusing Censorship: The Librarian's Guide to Handling Censorship Conflicts*. Phoenix, AZ: Oryx Press, 1983.

Information about court cases pertaining to censorship in schools, school libraries, and public libraries.

CENSORSHIP: THE SEARCH FOR THE OBSCENE*

Censorship, intellectual freedom, the student's right to read/listen/view materials—these are perennial topics of debate for librarians. For your next discussion group, seminar, or workshop, consider responding to the following statements and discussing the results with your colleagues.

Courts in the United States and England have addressed themselves to all of the following points in attempting to define obscenity. Judges have agreed and disagreed on all of the statements. You are being asked to state your opinion, not to answer according to what you think the law is, or has been.

Considerations	Agree	Disagree
1. The motive of the author is vital in deciding whether a work is obscene.	____	____
2. The reputation of the author should be a major consideration in the decision.	____	____
3. The esteem in which critics hold the work is important.	____	____
4. A work that is very expensive and thus likely to reach only a few people does not have to meet the same standards for obscenity as those in cheap editions, available to many people.	____	____
5. Protection of youth must take precedence over adult interests.	____	____
6. Some themes, e.g. homosexuality, are automatically obscene regardless of how they are handled.	____	____
7. There is a difference between vulgarity and obscenity.	____	____
8. Certain words are obscene regardless of the context in which they appear.	____	____
9. A work that leads the reader to have sexually impure or lustful thoughts is obscene.	____	____
10. A work should be judged by its possible effect on 'the well-regulated mind.'	____	____
11. A work should be judged by its possible effect on the abnormal people in society.	____	____
12. Words and scenes which in themselves are obscene by any definition are acceptable when their purpose is to provide relevance to the thoughts and actions of the characters and not to promote lust and filth for their own sake.	____	____
13. A work may be offensive to many without being obscene.	____	____

*Reprinted with permission from *Emergency Librarian,* subscriptions to which are available for $25 from Dyad Services, P.O. Box 46258, Station G, Vancouver, British Columbia V6R 4G6. This form was developed by the Book and Periodical Council of Canada and printed in *Emergency Librarian.*

<u>Considerations</u> (continued)

	Agree	Disagree
14. Material that appears in a nonfiction work designed to inform is held to different standards than fiction which is designed for the amusement of the reader.	_____	_____
15. Professionals (in medicine and science, for example) have a right to materials that are patently and obviously obscene.	_____	_____
16. Movies have a greater capacity for evil effects and are subject to different standards than printed materials.	_____	_____
17. Motion pictures are as important as books to our culture.	_____	_____
18. The phrase 'community standards' should be applied to the nation as a whole.	_____	_____
19. The phrase 'community standards' should be applied to a state/province as a whole.	_____	_____
20. The phrase 'community standards' should be applied to each individual town/ city.	_____	_____
21. Materials that lead people to think bad thoughts are as objectionable as those that lead to action.	_____	_____
22. Local groups do not violate anyone's freedom by organizing to remove materials they consider objectionable from their communities.	_____	_____
23. Newspapers and magazines are within their rights in refusing to take ads when the publishers disagree with the ad content.	_____	_____
24. Pornography should be protected under the U.S. First Amendment/Canadian Bill of Rights.	_____	_____
25. Radio and television should be held to different (e.g. higher) standards of morality than print materials.	_____	_____

Most (if not all) answers can be found by reading *Censorship: The Search for the Obscene* by Morris Ernst and Allan Schwartz, Macmillan, 1964. It is no longer up-to-date in terms of recent U.S. Supreme Court decisions, but is still one of the best around. [This form was developed by Dorothy Broderick.]

■ *Dorothy Broderick is Associate Professor at the Graduate School of Library Science, University of Alabama and Co-Editor of Voice of Youth Advocates.*

■■ **Alternate Activities for the Workshop** ■■

WHO ARE THE COMPLAINANTS? WHAT ARE THEY SAYING?

You can substitute this activity for the role plays or case studies. The following list of resources includes the views of different complainants concerning objectionable library materials. The group can read one article or read or listen to excerpts from a number of the materials to get the complainants' views. The participants can discuss their reactions in one large group, or they can divide into small groups of six to eight people. Participants can also discuss how they would handle such a complaint.

Resources

"Are Libraries Fair? Pre-Selection Censorship in a Time of Resurgent Conservatism." *Newsletter on Intellectual Freedom* 31 (September 1982): 151, 181–85. (Audiocassette available from the American Library Association, #82/010, $10.95.)

> Remarks by Cal Thomas, vice president of the Moral Majority, delivered at the 1982 ALA Annual Conference in Philadelphia.

"Censorship in the Eighties." *Drexel Library Quarterly* 18 (Winter 1982).
> Articles dealing with the new Christian Right and the Moral Majority.

Censorship or Selection: Choosing Books for Public Schools. Media and Society Seminars, 1982. 60 min. $150.00. ¾" videocassette. (Available from Barbara Eddings, Media and Society Seminars, 204 Journalism, Columbia University, New York, NY 10027.)
> Panel discussion that includes officers of the Moral Majority, teachers, principals and superintendents, a tenth-grade student, librarians, school board members, community activists, publishers, and authors Kurt Vonnegut and Judy Blume. This videocassette could also be substituted for the keynote speaker.

"The Criticizing of Racism and Sexism by the Council on Interracial Books for Children Is Not Censorship: Pro and Con." *English Journal* 70 (September 1981): 14–19.
> A series of short position papers that explore diverse opinions on selection guidelines versus censorship.

Hentoff, Nat. "When Nice People Burn Books." *The Progressive* 42 (February 1983): 42–44.
> A documentation of censorship attempts from liberal groups. Upholds the rights of freedom of speech and expression for all viewpoints.

"Intellectual Freedom in the '80s: The Impact of Conservatism." *Newsletter on Intellectual Freedom* 30 (November 1981): 148, 173–78. (Audiocassettes available from the American Library Association, #81/031, #81/032, #81/033, all for $32.85)
> Address by Michael Farris, executive director and general legal counsel of the Moral Majority of Washington State, delivered at the 1981 ALA Annual Conference.

Jenkinson, Edward B. *Censors in the Classroom: The Mind Benders*. Carbondale: Southern Illinois University Press, 1979.
> A discussion of textbook controversies, book battles, secular humanism, and other concerns of those objecting to school and library materials.

Kilpatrick, James. "Common Sense and Censorship." *Nation's Business* 70 (June 1982): 12.
> Editorial urging compromise in the area of intellectual freedom.

"Man the Bookshelves." *60 Minutes. CBS News Index* Microfiche Collection, 14 (November 1, 1981): 2–6.
> A transcript of a *60 Minutes* program which includes a fundamentalist minister challenging books in the Washington County Public Library in Abingdon, Virginia.

Oboler, Eli M., ed. "Censorship and Education." *The Reference Shelf* 53 (1981).
> A description of groups and individuals espousing both conservative and liberal views who have lodged complaints against textbooks and library materials.

———. "The Controversy Surrounding Values Education." *School Library Journal* 27 (October 1980): 115–17.
> An overview of some of the key issues and pertinent court cases.

What Shall They Read? Pacifica Archive Record, n.d.
60 min. Recording.

> A recording of a public hearing before the Richmond, California, City Council on the banning of underground newspapers and other materials from the public library.

CENSORSHIP VERSUS SELECTION

You can also substitute this activity for the role plays or case studies. The following list of resources represents different views on censorship versus selection, as well as self-censorship by librarians. The group can read one article and discuss it. Or small groups can read and discuss different articles and report to the group as a whole. If only one or two articles are to be discussed, you might mail the articles to participants before the workshop so they can read and think about them ahead of time. Allow time in the workshop for everyone to review the articles before discussion, since not everyone will have read the articles. Bring extra copies of the articles because some people may forget to bring their copies with them.

Resources

Nocera, Joseph. ''The Big Book-Banning Brawl.'' *New Republic* 187 (September 13, 1982): 20–25.

> A discussion of the Pico case. Suggests that public libraries and school libraries should approach censorship issues somewhat differently.

Swan, John C. ''Librarianship Is Censorship.'' *Library Journal* 104 (October 1, 1979): 2040–43.

> An examination of the paradoxes involved in the librarian's role ''as a censor who must fight censorship.''

Woods, L. B., and Perry-Holmes, Claudia. ''The Flak if We Had *The Joy of Sex* Here.'' *Library Journal* 107 (September 15, 1982): 1711–15.

> The results of a survey of public librarians in the United States which examined self-censorship.

To stimulate discussion on how librarians' personal values affect selection decision, you might use the group exercise in Judith W. Powell and Robert B. LeLieuvre's *Peoplework: Communications Dynamics for Librarians* (Chicago: American Library Association, 1979), entitled ''Individual Affective Selection Criteria.'' This exercise asks participants to rank 12 books in priority order for purchase and then to identify which selections would constitute the most risk in terms of citizen or board member objections. The group discusses the reasons for their choices and their thoughts about the selection process.

■ Additional Resources for the Workshop ■

COLLECTION DEVELOPMENT POLICIES AND PROCEDURES FOR HANDLING COMPLAINTS

Librarians need a written and approved collection development or selection policy and written procedures for handling citizen complaints. The following references will assist participants in developing their policies and procedures and in reviewing existing documents.

Basic Components of a Public Library Collection Development Policy. Baltimore: Maryland Library Association, 1981. ERIC document ED 220 103.

Foley, Robert. "The Community's Role in Dealing with Censorship." *Educational Leadership* 40 (January 1983): 51–54.

Futas, Elizabeth, ed. *Library Acquisition Policies and Procedures.* 2nd ed. Phoenix, AZ: Oryx Press, 1984.
    Sample policies from public libraries.

Jones, Frances M. *Defusing Censorship: The Librarian's Guide to Handling Censorship Conflicts.* Phoenix, AZ: Oryx Press, 1983.
    Note especially Chapters 10—"Internal Censorship: Putting Principles into Practice"; 11—"Responsible Planning and Effective Response: Meeting the Challenge of Censorship"; and Appendix 1—"Sample Policies and Guidelines" (for public and school libraries).

Policies and Procedures for Selection of Instructional Materials. Chicago: American Association of School Librarians, 1977.

Stahlschmidt, Agnes D. "A Democratic Procedure for Handling Challenged Library Materials." *School Library Media Quarterly* 11 (Spring 1983): 200–03.
    An article describing the inclusion of community members and high school students on committees that handle challenges to books and instructional materials in Iowa school districts.

Taylor, Mary M., ed. *School Library and Media Center Acquisitions Policies and Procedures.* Phoenix, AZ: Oryx Press, 1981.

Zenke, Larry L. *School Book Selection: Procedures, Challenges, and Responses.* Paper presented at the Annual Meeting of the National Council of Teachers of English, Boston, MA., November 20–25, 1981. ERIC document ED 213 022.
    Policy on academic freedom from the Tulsa, Oklahoma, Board of Education, outlining the rights and responsibilities of the school, educators, students, and parents.

STATE HANDBOOKS

Some state library associations, state libraries, and state education agencies have published handbooks that contain sample selection policies and procedures for dealing with citizen complaints, reprints of the ALA intellectual freedom statements, textbook adoption procedures, and lists of state intellectual freedom groups. Contact your state library association to find out whether such a handbook is available for your state.

Florida Library Association, Intellectual Freedom Committee. *Florida Intellectual Freedom Manual.* Tallahassee, FL: Florida Library Association, 1982. (Available from Florida Library Association, 2411 Winthrop Rd., Tallahassee, FL 32312. $2.10.)

Indiana State Teachers Association. *Censorship: Professional Improvement Packet.* Indianapolis: Indiana State Teachers Association, 1979. ERIC document ED 193 749.

Maryland Library Association. *Basic Components of a Public Library Collection Development Policy.* Baltimore, MD: Maryland Library Association, 1981. ERIC document ED 220 103.

Michigan Library Association, Intellectual Freedom Committee. *Handbook on Intellectual Freedom.* Lansing, MI: Michigan Library Association, 1982. (Available from Michigan Library Association, 226 W. Washtenaw, Lansing, MI 48933.)

Ohio Educational Library/Media Association, Intellectual Freedom Department. *School Libraries and Intellectual Freedom.* Columbus, OH: OELMA, 1982. (Available from OELMA Office, 40 South Third Street, Suite 409, Columbus, OH 43215. $3.00.)

Rhode Island Library Association. *Intellectual Freedom Handbook,* Rev. ed. Providence, RI: Rhode Island Library Association, 1982. (Available from Melody Brown, Department of State Library Services, 95 Davis St., Providence, RI 02908. $2.95.)

Texas Library Association, Committee on Intellectual Freedom and Professional Responsibilities. *TLA Information Handbook,* 2nd ed. Houston, TX: Texas Library Association, 1982. (Available from Texas Library Association, 8989 Westheimer, Suite 108, Houston, TX 77063. $.75.)

NONPRINT MATERIALS

There are a number of nonprint materials on intellectual freedom. Before you decide to use any of these items, however, preview the presentation to be sure that it fits your workshop objectives and that it contributes to what you want participants to learn. For the most effective use of nonprint media, introduce the presentation with key questions or ideas that you want participants to note. Then follow up with a discussion of the key points and a chance for participants to discuss how the presentation relates to their particular concerns about intellectual freedom.

If you choose to use any nonprint media, you must arrange for the equipment needed to show the item during the workshop. The following article gives excellent instructions on setting up and "debugging" different types of audiovisual equipment before presentations: Challis, A. James, and Alley, Brian. "Can You Hear Me at the Back of the Room?" *Technicalities* 2 (July 1982): 12–15.

The following may be used in place of the "Censorship Quiz" to introduce the workshop.

Banned Books—Censorship and Its Implications for Libraries. Emporia State University, School of Library Science, 1981. 20 min. Slide-tape presentation. (Available on loan from: School of Library and Information Management, Emporia State University, Emporia, KS 66801.)

A program on the history of book censorship in America, as well as present concerns.

The following two nonprint items may be used in place of the keynote speaker. One is appropriate for a school audience, the other, a public library group.

Censorship or Selection: Choosing Books for Public Schools. Media and Society Seminars, 1982. 60 min. $150.00. ¾" videocassette. (Available from: Barbara Eddings, Media and Society Seminars, 204 Journalism, Columbia University, New York, NY 10027.)

A panel discussion from the 1982 Conference of the National School Board Association focusing on required classroom reading; the selection, use, and removal of school library materials; and the legality of teaching scientific creationism in the public school curriculum. Panel members include authors Kurt Vonnegut and Judy Blume.

Freedom in America: The Two-Century Record. American Library Association, Office for Intellectual Freedom, 1978. 24 min. $65.00. 2 filmstrips, 2 audiocassettes, and discussion guide.

Introduces the basic legal concepts of the First Amendment (freedom of speech and the press) and the history of freedom of expression from the colonial era to the present.

CASE STUDIES

If you want to use case studies in your censorship workshop, but you do not want to use the case studies included in this manual (see Part IV), the following are sources for additional case studies.

Anderson, A. J. *Problems in Intellectual Freedom and Censorship.* New York: Bowker, 1974.

Case studies from all types of libraries.

Jones, Frances M. *Defusing Censorship: The Librarian's Guide to Handling Censorship Conflicts.* Phoenix, AZ: Oryx Press, 1983.

  Contains details of actual censorship cases in public and school libraries.

"Man the Bookshelves." *60 Minutes. CBS News Index,* Microfiche Collection, 14 (November 1, 1981): 2–6.

  Transcript of the *60 Minutes* television program that included the censorship controversy at the Washington County Public Library in Abingdon, Virginia.

Robotham, John, and Shields, Gerald. *Freedom of Access to Library Materials.* New York: Neal-Schuman, 1982.

  Includes a case study of censorship in a school library media center.

Shuman, Bruce A. *The River Bend Casebook: Problems in Public Library Service.* Phoenix, AZ: Oryx Press, 1981.

  Includes cases that deal with censorship problems in a public library—use of meeting rooms, library programing, and objectionable materials.

Part IV
Materials for the Workshop

3. In your opinion, what harmful effects might result from the use of this item? _____

_____

_____

4. Do you see any value in the use of this item? (Instructional, literary, self-development?) _____

_____

5. Should the opinion of any additional experts in the field be considered? If yes, please list suggestions.

_____

_____

6. In the place of this item, would you care to recommend other material which you consider to be of equal of superior quality for the purpose intended? _____

_____

_____

7. Do you wish to make an oral presentation to the review committee? _____

_____   _____

       DATE   SIGNATURE

Procedures for Reconsideration of Materials

If a complaint is made, the following procedures should be followed:

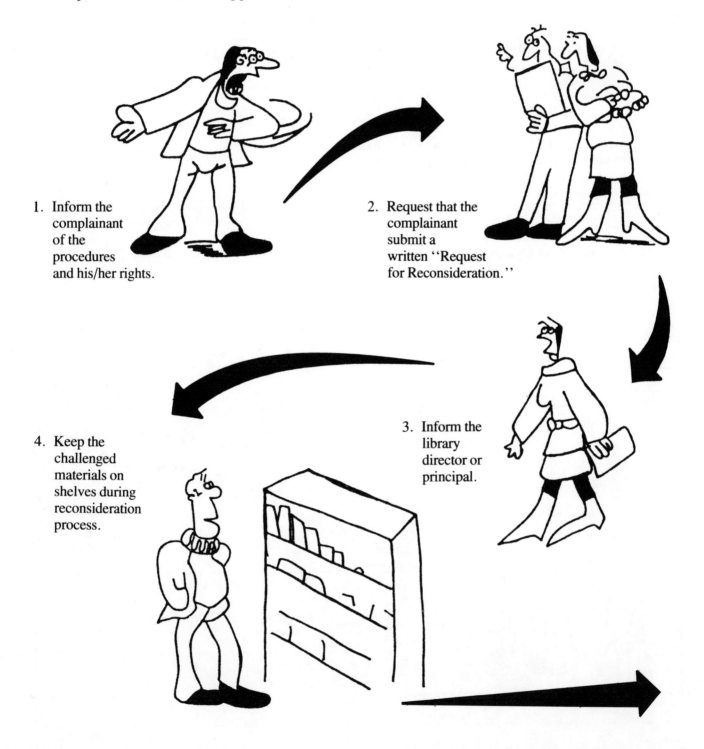

1. Inform the complainant of the procedures and his/her rights.

2. Request that the complainant submit a written "Request for Reconsideration."

3. Inform the library director or principal.

4. Keep the challenged materials on shelves during reconsideration process.

5. Form a committee to review the materials.

6. The review committee takes the following steps:
   a. reads, views, or listens to the material;
   b. checks general acceptance of the material by reading reviews and consulting recommended lists;
   c. determines the extent to which the material fits the selection policy;
   d. files a written report.

7. Present recommendations of review committee to the library director or principal and the board.

8. The principal or library director then tells the complainant the decision.

Case Study Summaries

The workshop leader may use these summaries for group discussion, or s/he may choose to distribute this handout to participants to summarize the case studies that they did not read.

CASE STUDY I: Use of the Meeting Room (Public Library)

When the Gay and Lesbian Rights Alliance plans to use the meeting room for a program, the director can see no reason to deny their request. Now she is receiving strong disapproval from the community that may jeopardize the branch library building program.

1. Given that you have granted permission, what would you do now?

2. What techniques for mobilizing community support would you suggest?

CASE STUDY II: A Citizen's Complaint (Public Library)

The director of the public library receives a letter from an irate citizen who has not found books recommended by the Moral Majority in the public library. The director wonders whether his own personal liberal biases have affected his selection decisions.

1. How would you respond to the citizen's letter?

2. How do your values affect the selection decisions that you make?

CASE STUDY III: Removal of Sexist Materials (School Library Media Center)

A media specialist in a middle school proposes to weed sexist materials from the school media center at the strong recommendation of some of the teachers.

1. As director of the media center, what is your response?

2. What is the role of the school media center in educating young people about the serious consequences of sex role stereotyping?

CASE STUDY IV: Parents' Rights (School Library Media Center)

A parent objects to a sex education book in an elementary school library media center on the basis that the book presents explicit sex without moral values and that parents have the right to make decisions about their children's reading material.

1. Discuss parents' rights in the context of children's rights to access library materials.

2. How would you respond to the parent?

◼◼◼ Case Study I: Use of the Meeting Room ◼◼◼

The Central City Public Library's auditorium/meeting room has been heavily used by community groups for their regular meetings and for community programs. Programs occur three to four times per week and reflect a diversity of interests—folk dancing, foreign films, travel series, book discussion groups, retirement planning, communications skills, and job skills for young adults. The library promotes the use of the meeting room as a community facility, a place where groups may meet for a nominal fee. The room seats 150 people.

Central City Public Library's meeting room policy, as follows, has been in effect for five years.

CENTRAL CITY PUBLIC LIBRARY
POLICY ON THE USE OF THE LIBRARY MEETING ROOM

As a public institution dedicated to free expression and free access to ideas representing all points of view concerning the problems and issues of our times, the Central City Public Library makes its meeting room available to any group of citizens of Central City whose purpose is not illegal and whose conduct is not objectionable, subject to the following regulations:

1. The meeting room may be used only during the regular hours of the library.

2. No fees, dues, or donations may be charged or solicited by the user for any program or exhibit. All programs and exhibits shall be free.

3. All programs and exhibits shall be open to the public.

4. Booking will come on a first come, first served basis.

5. A nonrefundable $15 fee is charged to compensate the library's custodial staff for overtime spent in cleaning up.

6. The room must be reserved at least 7 days in advance by written application in the library business office.

7. Refreshments may be served, but no alcoholic beverages and no smoking are permitted.

8. Children's groups must be supervised by at least one adult.

9. Each group using the room must sign a statement accepting responsibility for damage or loss of library equipment or furnishings.

10. Granting permission to use library facilities does not constitute an endorsement by the library staff or board of the group or its beliefs.

Elaine Smith, the library director, has had no occasion to question this policy until recently. Two weeks earlier, John Newcomb and Susan Dewar, coordinators of the Gay and Lesbian Rights Alliance in Central City, had requested the use of the library meeting room for the evening of Wednesday, April 12, to present a program for the public on gay and lesbian life styles. The Gay and Lesbian Rights Alliance had met all the regulations stipulated in the library policy, and so the program had been scheduled.

Elaine Smith is somewhat nervous about scheduling the program, however. While she believes strongly in the public library as a forum for community issues and as the place where all views can be read, heard, and discussed, she fears that this program could become controversial because of recent events in Central City.

The Gay and Lesbian Rights Alliance has become very visible since it was formed two years ago to protest the firing of an elementary school teacher who is a homosexual. Recently, the Gay and Lesbian Rights Alliance has been fighting to defeat a proposed housing ordinance that would allow landlords to discriminate against potential tenants based on their sexual preference. The heavy media coverage of AIDS (Acquired Immune Deficiency Syndrome) has also caused an increased backlash against the gay community.

• • •

As soon as the program was announced in the newspaper, Elaine Smith—as well as the library board members and the Mayor—began receiving telephone calls and letters from upset and angry community residents who demanded that the program be cancelled. The following Letter to the Editor appeared in the newspaper:

Dear Editor:

I'm appalled that the Central City Public Library would support that Homosexual Group. Those people have caused enough trouble in our city! We certainly don't want to encourage them to talk about their sinful and disgusting life. They should be hiding their faces in shame—not proselytizing our young people from a public meeting room. I call on the Mayor to stop this meeting from taking place.

An editorial in the local newspaper called for the library to cancel the program and stop supporting the "immoral and dangerous homosexual element in our fine city."

The chair of the library board and the city manager are now both concerned about the loss of public support and credibility for the library, especially at this time. In one month, a bond election will be held for a branch library building program in a retirement community and in a lower income neighborhood. These issues are being discussed and these questions are being asked at the library board meeting:

• Why jeopardize library service and new branches that would serve community residents who are currently not being adequately served in the central library building?

• Why can't we ask the Gay and Lesbian Rights Alliance to postpone the program until after the bond election?

• The homosexual group represents only a negligible percentage of the city's population—maybe the library has inadvertently become involved in a political issue.

• We certainly can't take sides or support only one side of a controversial issue.

QUESTIONS

1. Do you agree with Elaine Smith's decision to allow the Gay and Lesbian Rights Alliance to hold a program in the library? What about the library board's concerns?

2. What options does the Central City Public Library have now, given that the program has been scheduled and publicized?

3. What would you recommend to the library board?

4. How can the library reestablish credibility in the community and mobilize support for its decision?

■ Case Study II: A Citizen's Complaint ■

The Midland Public Library serves the city of Midland (75,000) and the surrounding rural Hays County (25,000). The library director, Ken Bond, is young, enthusiastic, and prides himself on a collection that addresses contemporary issues representing diverse viewpoints. He has a good relationship with his board and broad community support. The library is well-used by the community.

Ken has just received the following letter from a prominent local businessman.

Dear Mr. Bond,

I have always respected and valued the wisdom and knowledge available in libraries. Libraries are Everyman's University. They should contain the truth and enlightenment needed to guide our community during these troubled times.

You can imagine my dismay when I browsed through your library yesterday looking for books that were recommended in a recent issue of the *Moral Majority Report*. I could find only five from a list of over fifty books! But on those same shelves are such un-American and immoral books as *The Joy of Gay Sex* and *Our Bodies, Ourselves;* books hailing values clarification as a replacement for God; books on the dangerous practice of natural healing; and more books by women's libbers than I ever knew existed. I'm shocked! Where are the books supporting American values and the American way of life? Has America become so immoral, so decadent, that libraries no longer have books fit to be read by God-fearing men?

Your library needs my help. I intend to form a committee of concerned citizens to evaluate the library collection thoroughly. We will be back in touch with you. In the meantime, I have enclosed the list of recommended books from the *Moral Majority Report* so that you can begin purchasing these titles immediately.

John Bartholemew,
Vice President
First National Bank

Ken Bond is upset by the letter, because he thinks he works hard with his staff to select a balanced collection. He also realizes that the library's collection contains works whose content might be disturbing to some members of the community. However, Ken knows that the views of the Moral Majority are disturbing to *him,* and he wonders if he has decided not to purchase these materials because of his own personal feelings. He also wonders how the library board will react.

Ken looks through the list of books, which includes the following topics: the women's movement, the pro-life movement, conservative politics, drugs, creationism, homosexualtiy, defense, and family policy. He recognizes some of the titles that he has purchased for the library, and he is sure that the library owns more than five of the books that are listed. Some titles on the list are familiar to him but were not purchased because of poor reviews. Yet, he also notices many titles that are not in the library and that are from unfamiliar publishers. The list also includes periodicals and newsletters recommended by the Moral Majority. The library owns two of the six titles.

Ken Bond feels that it is imperative to write a letter to John Bartholemew immediately.

QUESTIONS

1. Draft a letter to John Bartholemew.

2. What else would you do in Ken Bond's situation?

3. If this letter were received by the high school library media specialist, would the response be different? In what ways?

4. How do your values affect the selection decisions that you make?

Case Study III: Removal of Sexist Materials

It's the beginning of the school year at Southside Middle School. Joan Green has been the media specialist at the middle school for ten years. She is respected by faculty members and the school administration for her innovative work in integrating library learning experiences with assignments and for her enthusiasm and patience in working with young people. Joan has a new assistant library media specialist this year—Toni Moore, a recent library school graduate.

Toni is enjoying working with the faculty of the middle school, especially a group of young women teachers who share a common concern about the prevalence of sex role stereotypes and the harm caused to both women and men by these expectations. Yesterday at lunch Toni was discussing these concerns with some of the teachers. One of the teachers suggested that Toni could start by examining library materials for sexist stereotypes. Toni went back to the media center and found that the media center has excellent materials portraying girls and women in a variety of job situations as well as working in the home. There are also materials depicting women and girls participating in various sports and leading active lives. The media center also has current books portraying boys and men in a variety of roles, including working in the home and nurturing children. However, Toni has found some sexist materials that include outdated stereotypes of women and girls—most of which were published ten or more years ago.

Toni approaches Joan Green, her supervisor. Toni feels strongly that it's harmful to expose young people to materials that reinforce negative stereotypes of women. The schools should take the lead to remove these stereotypes. Toni is enthusiastic about taking on the project of weeding the media center of the outdated sexist material. Some of the teachers have volunteered to spend three hours a week helping her until the project is complete. Toni is ready to start immediately.

QUESTIONS

1. What is your response as Joan Green, the library media specialist?

2. What strategies can the school media center use to assist in educating young people about the serious consequences of sex role stereotyping?

3. What should Joan Green and Toni Moore do next?

▬▬ Case Study IV: Parents' Rights ▬▬

The Central Elementary School (with students from kindergarten through fifth grade) is located in a primarily middle class community, with some Black and Mexican-American families. The parents are active in the PTA and have been very supportive of the school in the past. The school library media specialist, Carol McClennon, has an excellent school media center. She is careful in her selection decisions, and she has a deep commitment to children's rights to access materials appropriate to their reading and interest levels.

Mrs. Jean Simmons, the president of the Central Elementary School PTA, has recently discovered a book in the elementary school media center that she finds disturbing. The book is Stephanie Waxman's *Growing Up Feeling Good: A Child's Introduction to Sexuality* (Panjandrum, 1979), written for children, preschool through fourth grade. Mrs. Simmons objects to the following items:

1. Photographs of frontal nudity of male and female adolescents.

2. Photographs of couples making love.

3. Explicit descriptions of sexual behavior without discussion of moral values.

Mrs. Simmons has filed a formal complaint and has asked that the book be removed from the library immediately, or at least placed on a restricted shelf so that only parents and teachers can check out the book. In addition to the specific complaints about the content of the book, Mrs. Simmons has this to say about her rights as a parent:

"This school library has no right to give my third-grade son such a book without my knowledge or consent. It is not right that my child be exposed to things in this library that I strenuously object to. He's my child—not the library's. I want to be the guide of my child's sexual understanding and growing up. I have very definite values that I want to impart to my child. This is my responsibility. I do not want to delegate it—or have it taken from my hands—by the school. Ms. McClennon, you have shown great concern for having books in the library that represent different roles for women and those that contain a sensitive and realistic portrayal of members of minority groups. I ask only that you show the same sensitivity to the feelings of people who believe in traditional morality. I think every group is entitled to legitimate and sensitive consideration of its feelings."

Ms. McClennon had based her decision to buy the book on a positive review in *School Library Journal*, which indicated that this was one of the few books on sexuality for children in which "sex is treated as a natural part of a continuum that involves responsibility and caring for others." Furthermore, the review praises the "sensitive and joyous photographs" depicting all ages and races of people. Other reviews were equally positive. In addition, the book had been recommended by one of the science teachers who teaches the sex education curriculum.

QUESTIONS

1. Review the book, if possible, and evaluate its appropriateness for an elementary school.

2. Discuss Mrs. Simmons' statements regarding parents' rights to make decisions about their children's reading materials.

3. How would you respond to Mrs. Simmons?

What to Do in Your Community*

Directions: Check activities you need to work on in your own library or school. Use the space under each question to make notes on who needs to be involved, what you'd like to do, and your timetable for accomplishing your goals.

_____ 1. Do you have a written materials selection policy?

_____

_____

Has it been formally adopted by your governing agency?

_____

_____

Is it revised and updated regularly?

_____

_____

_____ 2. Does your policy include a written procedure for handling complaints?

_____

_____

_____ 3. For school library media centers, are board members, central administrators, teachers, and support staff aware of the contents of your materials selection policy?

_____

_____

_____ 4. For public libraries, are all library staff, volunteers, and board members aware of your materials selection policy?

_____

_____

_____ 5. Do you have open communication lines with civic, religious, educational, and political bodies in your community?

_____

_____

_____ 6. Do you encourage your district or your public library board to maintain a vigorous public relations program on behalf of intellectual freedom?

_____

_____

*Idea taken from: *Censorship: Professional Improvement Packet*. Indianapolis: Indiana State Teachers Association, 1979. ERIC document ED 193 749.

_____ 7. Do you have a good relationship with the news media in your community—newspaper and television reporters, newspaper editors, and radio announcers?

_____

_____

_____ 8. For school personnel, have you prepared written rationales for using specific classroom materials, especially those that students are *required* to use to meet educational objectives?

_____

_____ 9. Are you aware of groups in your community who are likely to initiate complaints about library and instructional materials?

_____

_____

_____ 10. Are you aware of groups in your community who are advocates of intellectual freedom and who might have resources they would enlist in your support?

_____

_____

_____ 11. Are you aware of state and national organizations that are advocates of intellectual freedom?

_____

_____

■ **Where to Get Help** ■

NATIONAL GROUPS

American Association of School Librarians
50 E. Huron St.
Chicago, IL 60611
(312) 944-6780

American Library Association
Office for Intellectual Freedom
50 E. Huron St.
Chicago, IL 60611
(312) 944-6780

American Civil Liberties Union
22 E. 40th St.
New York, NY 10016
(212) 944-9800

Association of American Publishers
1 Park Ave.
New York, NY 10016
(212) 689-8920

First Amendment Lawyer's Association
Suite 1200
1737 Chestnut St.
Philadelphia, PA 19108
(215) 665-1600

National Coalition against Censorship
132 W. 43rd St.
New York, NY 10036
(212) 944-9899

National Council of Teachers of English
1111 Kenyon Rd.
Urbana, IL 61801
(217) 328-3870

National Education Association
1201 16th St., N.W.
Washington, DC 20036
(202) 833-4000

LOCAL AND STATE GROUPS

Directions: Use this worksheet as a guide to compile a list of local and state groups involved in intellectual freedom. Include the name, address, telephone number, and name of a contact person, if possible, for each of the following groups in your state.

State Library Association: _____

Address

_____ _____

Phone   Contact Person

State Library Association, Intellectual Freedom Committee: _____

Address

_____ _____

Phone   Contact Person

State Media Specialists' Association: _____

Address

_____ _____

Phone   Contact Person

State Education Association: _____

Address

_____ _____

Phone   Contact Person

State Library: _____

Address

_____ _____

Phone   Contact Person

State Department of Education: _____

Address

_____ _____

Phone   Contact Person

Regional Library Systems: _____

Address

_____ _____

Phone   Contact Person

Educational Service Centers: _____

Address

_____ _____

Phone   Contact Person

School of Library Science: _____

Address

_____ _____

Phone   Contact Person

■ **For More Information** ■

Berninghausen, David K. "The Arrogance of the Censor." *USA Today* 110 (March 1982): 61–63.

Good summary of current concerns, with historical perspective.

———. "Intellectual Freedom in Librarianship: Advances and Retreats." *Advances in Librarianship* 9 (1979): 1–29.

Overview of intellectual freedom issues in all types of libraries.

Bosmajian, Haig A. *Censorship, Libraries, and the Law*. New York: Neal-Schuman, 1983.

A source that includes lower court decisions about censorship in libraries, as well as pertinent Supreme Court rulings.

Broderick, Dorothy M. "Censorship: A Family Affair?" *Top of the News* 35 (Spring 1979): 223–32.

A discussion of family values and lifestyles as these affect children's right to read and access to information.

———. *Library Work with Children*. New York: H. W. Wilson, 1977.

A source for information on collection development for children's materials, including selection standards, the controversy surrounding sexism and racism in children's materials, sex and sexuality, and the selection process.

"Censorship in the Eighties." *Drexel Library Quarterly* 18 (Winter 1982): 1–108.

Articles on the new Christian Right, the Moral Majority and popular political issues, self-censorship by librarians, intellectual freedom theory for users of libraries, and textbook censorship and intolerance in the classroom.

De Grazia, Edward, and Newman, Roger K. *Banned Films: Movie Censorship in the United States*. New York: Bowker, 1982.

Detailed history of film censorship in the United States from 1908 to 1981, with information about the 122 films that were banned.

Haight, Anne Lyon. *Banned Books: 387 B.C. to 1978 A.D.*, 4th ed. New York: Bowker, 1978.

A chronological list of banned books with some information on the controversy surrounding them, as well as excerpts from important court cases and selected U.S. laws and regulations.

Intellectual Freedom Manual, 2nd ed. Chicago: American Library Association, 1983.

The basic manual on combatting censorship; produced by the ALA Office for Intellectual Freedom.

Jones, Frances M. *Defusing Censorship: The Librarian's Guide to Handling Censorship Conflicts*. Phoenix, AZ: Oryx Press, 1983.

An excellent book for school and public librarians, giving current information about censorship conflicts that have occurred, recent court cases, and practical advice for handling censorship conflicts.

Newsletter on Intellectual Freedom. Bimonthly. American Library Association, 50 E. Huron St., Chicago, IL 60611. $15/year.

A periodical that explores censorship in all of its ramifications through articles, descriptions of censorship incidents throughout the U.S., and summaries of recent court rulings on freedom of the press and freedom of inquiry.

Norwick, Kenneth P. *Lobbying for Freedom in the 1980s: A Grass-Roots Guide*. New York: Putnam, 1983.

A book that presents effective lobbying techniques for enacting legislation to support your professional concerns, as a private citizen, on censorship.

VOYA (Voice of Youth Advocates). Bimonthly, April–February. Voice of Youth Advocates, Inc., PO Box 6569, University, AL 35486. $15/year.

A periodical that includes articles that focus on the right to information for children and young adults and provides book reviews of materials of interest to youth in the areas of sexuality, realistic fiction, and nonfiction dealing with the day-to-day concerns of children and youth.

Swan, John C. "Librarianship Is Censorship." *Library Journal* 104 (October 1, 1979): 2040–43.

> An article that examines the paradoxes involved in the librarian's role "as a censor who must fight censorship."

▬ Especially for Public Libraries ▬

Bundy, Mary Lee, and Stakem, Teresa. "Librarians and Intellectual Freedom: Are Opinions Changing?" *Wilson Library Bulletin* 56 (April 1982): 584–89.

> Results of a survey sent to public librarians about their attitudes toward intellectual freedom.

Futas, Elizabeth, ed. *Library Acquisition Policies and Procedures*. 2nd ed. Phoenix, AZ: Oryx Press, 1984.

> Sample selection policies from public libraries of different sizes.

Woods, L. B., and Perry-Holmes, Claudia. "The Flak if We Had *The Joy of Sex* Here." *Library Journal* 107 (September 15, 1982): 1711–15.

> Survey of public librarians to examine self-censorship.

■ Especially for Schools ■

Anderson, Philip, and Wetzel, Karen Lee. "A Survey of Legal Knowledge of High School Principals on Censorship Issues." *English Journal* 71 (February 1982): 34–39.

> Survey of Rhode Island principals indicating that many overestimate their own power in censorship decisions.

Censorship Litigation and the Schools. Chicago: American Library Association, 1983.

> Proceedings of a colloquium to analyze the opposition to First Amendment Rights, the proper duty of the state in shaping school curricula, and strategies for selecting and winning cases in the courts.

Davis, James E., ed. *Dealing with Censorship*. Urbana, IL: National Council of Teachers of English, 1979.

> A selection of articles aimed at the public schools.

Foley, Robert. "The Community's Role in Dealing with Censorship." *Educational Leadership* 40 (January 1983): pp. 51–54.

> A discussion of the current community-school conflicts involving intellectual freedom, describing procedures for handling citizen complaints effectively, and proposing that due process—not intellectual freedom—should be the basis of efforts to deal with censorship.

Kamhi, Michelle Marder. *Limiting What Students Shall Read: Books and Other Learning Materials in Our Public Schools—How They Are Selected and How They Are Removed*. Chicago: American Library Association, 1981.

> A study conducted jointly by the American Library Association, the Association for Supervision and Curriculum Development, and the Association of American Publishers.

Oboler, Eli M., ed. "Censorship and Education." *The Reference Shelf* 53 (6) (1981).

> Recent articles reprinted from library, education, publishing, and legal periodicals dealing with the climate of censorship, the censors, censorship in schools and libraries, and court decisions.

Policies and Procedures for Selection of Instructional Materials. Chicago: American Association of School Librarians, 1977.

> A booklet to assist in developing selection policy statements.

Stahlschmidt, Agnes D. "A Democratic Procedure for Handling Challenged Library Materials." *School Library Media Quarterly* 11 (Spring 1983): 200–03.

> An article describing the inclusion of community members and high school students on committees that handle challenges to books and instructional materials in Iowa school districts.

Sweet, William. "School Book Controversies." *Editorial Research Reports* (September 10, 1982): 673–92.

> Excellent current summary of the issues: challenges to assigned reading, responsibilities of educators and parents, complex reasons for citizen complaints, politics of textbook selection, and recent court cases.

Taylor, Mary M., ed. *School Library and Media Center Acquisitions Policies and Procedures*. Phoenix, AZ: Oryx Press, 1981.

> A source for selection policies and dealing with challenged materials.

What Can a Library Media Specialist Do to Preserve Intellectual Freedom? Chicago: American Association of School Librarians, 1982.

> Concise guidelines on the support of intellectual freedom, steps to follow if school library media center materials are challenged, and sources of help.

Zenke, Larry L. "School Book Selection: Procedures, Challenges, and Responses." Paper presented at the Annual Meeting of the National Council of Teachers of English, Boston, MA, November 20–25, 1981. ERIC document ED 213 022.

> Policy from the Tulsa, Oklahoma, Board of Education on academic freedom, which includes the school's responsibilities and the rights and responsibilities of educators, students, and parents.

Workshop Evaluation Form

_____ Public Librarian   _____ Teacher   _____ School Administrator
_____ School Library Media Specialist   _____ Trustee   _____ Other _____

1. Before this workshop, I: (Check all answers that apply)
   _____a. had experience in dealing with problems concerning intellectual freedom.
   _____b. had basic understanding of the principles of intellectual freedom.
   _____c. discussed the principles of intellectual freedom with other library staff, library trustees, and community residents.
   _____d. was unclear about my role in supporting intellectual freedom.
   _____e. felt uncomfortable with my role in supporting intellectual freedom.

	Uncomfortable			Comfortable	
2. Now how comfortable do you feel with your role in supporting intellectual freedom?	1	2	3	4	5

Comments: _____

_____

3. How do you plan to use the information you gained today? _____

_____

4. Rate the following sessions of the workshop. Comments will be useful to workshop planners.

	poor				excellent
a. First morning session on intellectual freedom principles.	1	2	3	4	5

   Comments: _____

_____

b. Second morning session on procedures for handling complaints and role plays.	1	2	3	4	5

   Comments: _____

_____

c. Afternoon case studies.	1	2	3	4	5

   Comments: _____

_____

5. The one thing I liked best about the workshop: _____

_____

_____

6. What I would like to see changed about the workshop: _____

_____

_____

7. My overall evaluation of the workshop: <u>poor</u>   <u>excellent</u>

                                                    1   2   3   4   5

    Additional comments/suggestions: _____

_____

_____

_____

_____

Part V
Transparency Originals

▬ Instructions for Using Transparencies ▬

These transparencies will aid group discussion of the answers to the ''Censorship Quiz'' and the group's responses to the ''Intellectual Freedom Question-naire.'' Transparencies can be made on some types of copying machines, such as a Thermofax copier. Make a good photocopy of the following pages because photocopies usually produce clearer transparencies. Use the photocopy on a machine that makes transparencies.

Most schools, school district offices, university media centers, and some public libraries have equipment that can photocopy onto transparencies.

You can also present this information written on flip charts or on a chalkboard. Be sure that you print the information ahead of time and that it is large enough for the entire group to read.

▬ Censorship Quiz ▬▬▬▬▬▬▬

_____   1. Merriam-Webster New Collegiate
            Dictionary

_____   2. Little Black Sambo

_____   3. The Living Bible

_____   4. Leaves of Grass

_____   5. Sylvester and the Magic Pebble

_____   6. The Merchant of Venice

_____   7. The Adventures of Huckleberry Finn

_____   8. Slaughterhouse-Five

_____   9. For Whom the Bell Tolls

_____   10. On the Origin of Species

_____   11. Are You There God? It's Me, Margaret

_____   12. Ulysses

_____   13. Inner City Mother Goose

_____ 14. Gulliver's Travels

_____ 15. Candide

_____ 16. The Odyssey

_____ 17. Sports Illustrated

_____ 18. National Geographic

_____ 19. Jesus Christ Superstar

_____ 20. Soul on Ice

_____ 21. The Anarchist Cookbook

Intellectual Freedom Questionnaire

1. Any person has the right to read, view, or listen to anything.

2. Curse words not for 12 and younger.

3. Pictures showing sex.

4. Atheism banned.

5. Women as housewives only.

6. Communism desirable.

7. Derogatory view of Indians, Blacks, Orientals banned.

8. Obscene to one is okay to others.

9. Adolescent novels on safe subjects.

10. Violence okay on TV, etc.

11. U.S. mistakes okay to show in textbooks.

12. Rank from 1 (most dangerous) to 10 (least dangerous).

_____   Atheism
_____   Communism
_____   Cursing
_____   Explicit sex
_____   Homosexuality
_____   Obscenities
_____   Pornography
_____   Racial prejudice
_____   Sexual stereotyping
_____   Violence

■ Index ■